99 THOUGHTS

PARENTS

of TEENAGERS

THE TRUTH ON RAISING TEENAGERS

FROM PARENTS WHO HAVE BEEN THERE

WALT
MUELLER

99 Thoughts for Parents of Teenagers
The Truth on Raising Teenagers From Parents Who Have Been There

Credits
Author: Walt Mueller
Executive Developer: Nadim Najm
Chief Creative Officer: Joani Schultz
Editors: Rob Cunningham and Janis Sampson
Cover Art and Production: Jeff Storm and Veronica Lucas
Production Manager: DeAnne Lear

Unless otherwise indicated, all Scripture quotations are taken from the *LIVE Holy Bible*, New Living Translation, copyright © 1996, 2004, 2007. Used by permission of Tyndale House Publishers, Inc., Carol Stream, Illinois 60188. All rights reserved.

Scripture quotations marked The Message are taken from *The Message*. Copyright © 1993, 1994, 1995, 1996, 2000, 2001, 2002. Used by permission of NavPress Publishing Group.

Scripture quotations marked Phillips are taken from *The New Testament in Modern English*, copyright © 1958, 1959, 1960 J.B. Phillips and 1947, 1952, 1955, 1957 The Macmillian Company, New York. Used by permission. All rights reserved.

ISBN 978-0-7644-4869-0

10 9   20 19 18 17 16 15 14

Printed in the United States of America.

DEDICATION

To the glory of God, with thanks to him for those who have filled my life and home with great joy: Lisa, Caitlin, Josh, Bethany, and Nate.

CONTENTS

INTRODUCTION

Once upon a time, I was the perfect parent—and then I got married and had kids. As time went on and our kids grew, I learned more and more about the realities of being a parent. I also realized how much I *didn't* know. I know I'm not alone. It's out of these realizations, my 27 years of experience as a parent of four kids (15 of those years spent parenting teenagers), and my years of work with parents and teenagers through the Center for Parent/Youth Understanding (cpyu.org) that this little book has been birthed.

But before you start reading, there are some more things you need to know about this book and me.

First, even though my name is on the cover, I'm not the only one who has "written" the words you'll find on the pages that follow. More than anything else, this is the result of a parenting collaboration with my wife, Lisa. Everything you read was learned, discussed, and thought about *together* over the course of our years as parents. Some of it we learned by studying the Bible,

God's Word. Some we learned in the classroom of experience. Some we learned just by living with kids. Other things were learned through our interactions with other parents and in the company of friends. In many ways, I'm just the guy who put the words on paper.

Second, we are painfully aware of the fact that we don't have it all figured out. If you picked this book up hoping to find fool-proof advice from parenting experts who have it all together, you're going to be very, very disappointed. Lisa and I are the first to say that we're "fellow strugglers" on this incredibly rewarding and sometimes frustrating journey of raising and relating to teenagers. The roof on our house covers a life-lab where many mistakes have been made by dad and mom. Thankfully, God is a God of great mercy and grace who uses our faults and shortcomings to do his work—in spite of who we are.

Third, we want to be transparent and honest. You need to know that we've had ups and downs in our parenting journey. Much of what you read has come out of our struggles to go deeper in our knowledge of God, our knowledge of ourselves, and our knowledge of who we are to be as parents. By the way, we're still in process on all those things!

Fourth, what you read is intended to be hope-filled. My desire is that no matter where you are in the parenting journey, you will find great hope and encouragement in the words you read. In many ways, I've simply passed on words that we've found helpful as parents of teenagers.

Finally, the little book you hold in your hands isn't anywhere near exhaustive. Think of it as a starter collection of thoughts that will help and encourage you along the way. I realize that I've probably left a lot out. There's so much more to parenting teenagers. My hope is that what you read here will whet your appetite in ways that will motivate you to go deeper by learning more.

A quick suggestion: Perhaps the best way to read this book is twice. Take some time to sit down and read it from cover to cover to get the big picture. Then go through it a second time, focusing on reading, pondering, and discussing one thought a day—prayerfully considering how God might be prompting you to work out and apply that thought in your home.

My prayer for you is that God would bless you as he parents you while you parent your teenagers. And may God use this little collection of thoughts to bear great fruit in the life of your family!

—Walt Mueller
Husband, father, fellow struggler, and founder and president of the Center for Parent/Youth Understanding (cpyu.org)

THE NON-NEGOTIABLES

1 TEENAGERS ARE A BLESSING, NOT A CURSE.

I will never forget the overwhelming wonder and amazing joy I felt when my first child (and all three since) was born. "I'm not worthy! What did I do to deserve this?" is what I cried out to God in gratitude for this great gift. Shortly thereafter, our daughter became a teenager. During my weaker moments, the challenges, confrontations, and difficulties sometimes left me asking God, "What have I done to deserve this?" Then I was reminded of Solomon's wise and truthful words: *Don't you see that children are God's best gift? the fruit of the womb his generous legacy? Like a warrior's fistful of arrows are the children of a vigorous youth. Oh, how blessed are you parents, with your quivers full of children! (Psalm 127:3-5 The Message).* Whether God graces you with easy parenting times or strengthens you during difficult parenting times, those children God gave you were gifts on the day they were born—and that hasn't changed! They still are.

2 GOD PARENTS YOU WHILE YOU PARENT YOUR CHILDREN.

Here's something that at first glance might be a scary thought for Christian parents: The Bible speaks from beginning to end about the presence and benefits of suffering. *Dear brothers and sisters, when troubles come your way, consider it an opportunity for great joy. For you know that when your faith is tested, your endurance has a chance to grow. So let it grow, for when your endurance is fully developed, you will be perfect and complete, needing nothing (James 1:2-4).* The teenage years bring difficulty for both teenagers and their parents. As a result, we can experience the joy of going deeper with God and depending on him during the challenges of adolescence. We've learned that the harder the difficulty, the deeper God is taking us. God wants us at the place where we drop our arms to our sides, look to him in desperation, and then confess, "OK, Lord, I've got nothing." Suffering is a process God uses to refine our children *and us* into his image and likeness. If we had to do it all over again as parents, would we change the circumstances that led us to suffering and helplessness? Absolutely not! It's been a gift that's taken us deeper in our dependence on him.

3 YOU'RE STILL IMPORTANT.

"Home is where the heart is." That cliché is a great descriptor of the way a little child's life revolves around family and home. Then the teenage years arrive and something begins to change. Because they are now growing up, teenagers begin the process of disengaging from the kind of ties they've had with you as they begin to focus more and more time on building relationships with their peers. Even though the shift is normal, it can be quite painful to watch your children trade family time for friend time. These new relationships with friends serve as a bridge between the dependence of childhood and the independence of adulthood. But never, never, never forget this fact: You are still vital! Research and observation have shown that we must remain engaged and available to our children. Teenagers whose parents are absent from their lives as a result of choice or circumstance are teenagers who hurt deeply. You are important and significant in their lives!

4 GUESS WHAT? YOU'VE GOT FAULTS...AND THEY NOW KNOW IT!

Remember what it was like when you figured out that your parents weren't the perfect, all-powerful, and all-knowing people that you once naively believed they were? If it hasn't happened already, your children will soon have that figured out about you. It's likely they won't hesitate to point out your faults on a regular basis. But don't let their treatment of you shape how you see yourself. While teenagers can be incredibly loving and compassionate, they can also be rude and insensitive for the simple fact that they are rather immature. (However, you might not want to point that out to them on a regular basis!) Realize that many of their remarks are the result of the confusion and impulsivity they're experiencing as they change and grow. Keep loving them. Keep treating them with Christ-like dignity and respect. Correct and discipline when necessary. And above all, let them know that, yep, they're right: You *are* a sinful and fallen parent with many, many faults. However, model the pursuit of Christ-likeness and dependence on his forgiving and redeeming grace. This, too, serves as a powerful opportunity to model the life of a Christ-follower.

5 ADMIT IT: THE TEENAGE YEARS ARE TOUGH!

It helped us to view our teenagers as people stuck in an earthquake—the earthquake known as adolescence. Think about it. The teen years arrive swiftly, pass rather quickly, and radically alter the landscape of a child's life. And just like real-life earthquakes, the earthquake of adolescence leaves its victims feeling all kinds of stress. They are juggling physical growth, new sexual urges, changing relationships, a host of new pressures, the quest for finding answers to a multitude of questions, and the desire to belong. Next time you're ready to throw in the parenting towel, picture your teenager struggling to live through the onset and aftermath of an earthquake. They need you now more than ever!

6 LIVE UNDER AND PROCLAIM THE AUTHORITY OF GOD'S WORD.

Have you ever thought about how and why we make the decisions we make? Every decision we make is based on some authority. Same thing goes for our children. It's highly likely that your teenagers, like most teenagers, rely *unconsciously* on some combination of authorities including peers, family, the media, and their feelings. While all of these authorities can lead us in the right direction and to good decisions, there is one primary authority we are called to live in *conscious* submission to. It's the authority of the One who formed us, made us, and desires us to find our rightful place in life in a relationship with him. Perhaps the greatest parental responsibility we have is to teach—

through our words and example—that all of life is to be lived under the authority of God. Our own eyes, ears, and lives must be focused on Jesus, who said, *"I have been given all authority in heaven and on earth" (Matthew 28:18),* and on God's revelation of himself in the Bible, which *is inspired by God and is useful to teach us what is true and to make us realize what is wrong in our lives. It corrects us when we are wrong and teaches us to do what is right (2 Timothy 3:16).* If this is the authority we live under, we'll be teaching the truth about their need to do the same.

SHOW THE GRACE YOU'VE BEEN SHOWN.

All teenagers face great temptation. All teenagers make sinful choices that are at times devastating to themselves and to others. It's who we are as human beings. And we've learned something else along the way: The most important factor in determining whether that bad choice turns into a situation that gets better or worse is parental response. What would happen if your goal would be to redeem these situations by turning a mistake into an opportunity for your teenager to become a more Christ-like person? I am constantly reminded of my responsibility to treat my sinful children the way my heavenly Father treats me when I'm the offending party—because there isn't a day that goes by when I'm not. I learned a great lesson from Dr. John White when he was asked about how he'd learned to relate to his own son's consistently rebellious and sinful choices. White simply said he'd learned to live his life according to this simple yet profound principle: "As Christ is to me, so must I be to my children."

8 PRAYER CHANGES THINGS— AND YOU'RE THE THING!

I once thought I knew quite a bit about raising children. Then I had them, and the older they grew, the less I realized I knew. You know what else I learned? That sometimes the place God wants us is in total dependence on him. That's the place where we need to pray for answers—answers to our questions about raising and relating to our teenagers. Paul's words became more and more real to me through the times of struggle I've faced as a parent: *Don't worry about anything; instead, pray about everything. Tell God what you need, and thank him for all he has done (Philippians 4:6).* Prayer is a wonderful gift God has given to us as we learn to depend on him and his power to keep us on track as dads and moms. And when we pray, we don't change God or his mind. Rather, the beauty of prayer is the change it brings in us.

9 PATIENCE IS A PRIMARY PARENTAL VIRTUE!

How easy it would be if adolescence were an overnight phenomena. But the process of moving from childhood to adulthood takes time. In today's world, the assumption that the adolescent years cease and a teenager becomes an adult at the age of 18 is no longer valid. New discoveries regarding the biochemistry and physiology of the human brain, along with a host of cultural forces (later marriage, extended college education, massive debt, living at home, delayed maturity) have fueled things like extended adolescence and emerging adulthood. Both are nice-sounding terms that when translated simply mean that our children are taking longer to grow up. Some are even wondering if adolescence extends to the age of 30! This process can be grueling and frustrating for those parents who desperately want to see their teenagers make good choices on the road to adulthood and arrive at the destination sooner rather than later. The tables turn, and we become the ones asking over and over, "Are we there yet?!?" Remember, God is at work and the process may take some time. Be patient!

10 EMBRACE THEIR SUFFERING.

It hurts—*a lot*—to watch your children suffer. In a youth culture pervaded by bullying, our teenagers may sometimes suffer injustice at the hands of others. Sometimes their suffering is brought on by choices they've made. At other times, circumstances related to illness or accidents are the cause of their suffering. Scripture teaches us that because of our sinful nature and the flawed nature of our world, we should not be surprised by difficulty and suffering. In fact, times of difficulty, pain, and suffering are what God uses to draw us to himself, to conform us to his likeness, and to whittle off all that extra "fluff" that keeps us from maturing in our faith. The psalmist knew this to be the case: *My suffering was good for me, for it taught me to pay attention to your decrees (Psalm 119:71).* James tells us that *when troubles come your way, consider it an opportunity for great joy (James 1:2).* Really? Why? Because this testing of our faith produces perseverance and maturity. When our teenagers suffer, it might actually be good for the simple reason that God is at work in their lives. While we want to see them thrive in lives free of hurt and pain, we shouldn't miss the opportunity to help them to learn, grow, and mature as they persevere through their suffering.

11 GOD IS GOD.

Parenting isn't easy. And as hard as we may try to protect our children from making bad decisions, they alone are responsible for their behavior. Unfortunately, many teenagers make decisions that are dangerous and can lead them down a difficult path. When this happens, our entire family is affected and it can often shake our faith to the core. We may wonder why God didn't protect our children or has allowed them to stray. But even our most spiritually mature teenagers make mistakes, and the results are often devastating. When this happens it is often good to remember the words of David: *"The foundations of law and order have collapsed. What can the righteous do?" But the Lord is in his holy Temple; the Lord still rules from heaven (Psalm 11:3-4).* Don't you love the way David answers that question? He simply recognizes that while everything else is crumbling, God remains. No matter how bad things seem to get, we need to remember that God is still God. God is sovereign. God is in control. Humans will fail us. Our children will disappoint us. But our heavenly Father is still seated firmly on his throne. Lock this truth away in the vault of your heart. Someday—if it hasn't happened already—you'll have nothing else to rest on but this truth.

12 ONE WORD: INTEGRITY.

The dictionary defines integrity as "firm adherence to a code of moral values" and "the quality of being complete or undivided." For Christians in our generation, compromise often comes in the form of putting on a good show for others, while living with lower standards and cutting corners in the "closets" of our lives—you know, those places we frequent where we think we are never seen by others. However, as parents of teenagers, we can be sure that our children's watchful eyes see more than we know or imagine. As a result, the emerging generation of children and teenagers has learned well from our example. So much so, in fact, even professing Christian teenagers today are less likely to even try hiding their duplicity. Integrity describes a life that is united in a complete and consistent whole. An integrated life is one where words, thoughts, and actions consistently reflect the will of God for our lives. It is a life where one's faith in God is woven in and through every area of life, including all that one does—even when no one else is looking. What can we do to counter the loss of integrity in today's youth culture and in the lives of our teenagers? First, take stock of your "closet" and take corrective action where necessary. Second, map out a lifestyle of 24/7 integrity where your faith intersects with and permeates *all* of life. Live out your faith in your marriage, vocation, play, media use, sexuality, conversation, intellectual pursuits, and every other area of life. And finally, map out a life of integrity for your children by pointing out and challenging their duplicity in the context of a loving and supportive relationship.

13 GOOD PARENTS DON'T ALWAYS RAISE GOD-HONORING CHILDREN.

A great amount of parental guilt has been fueled by taking the words of Proverbs 22:6 as a promise: *Direct your children onto the right path, and when they are older, they will not leave it.* The first half of that Proverb includes an imperative that we must follow. The responsibility we have to nurture our children in the faith is non-negotiable. But the result mentioned in the second half isn't, as we tend to think, a guarantee. Rather, it's a general statement about the way things may end up. The reality is that history and the world around us—maybe even the world in our own home—is filled with examples of wonderful, committed, diligent God-honoring parents whose first priority in life has been to train up their children in the way they should go, only to see some of those children choose to go in the opposite direction. The first father we read about in the Bible—God, the perfect Father—saw his first two children, Adam and Eve, rebel. There are many families where good parents have raised multiple children, some who have chosen the narrow path that leads to life, and others who have eagerly pursued the wider road that leads to destruction. What we can't forget is that ultimately, God's Spirit is the one responsible for bringing about the change in our children's hearts. We have no clue when that change may come. Our duty is to remain faithful and obedient in our calling as followers of Jesus who have been charged with the task of nurturing our children in the faith—regardless of their response to our efforts at any given point in time. And just as God continues to love his rebellious children, we need to do the same.

PARENTING TASKS

14 HELP THEM AS THEY LEARN TO "JUGGLE."

Over the years of raising my own children, I've learned to think about teenagers as jugglers. The older they get, they have to struggle to juggle more and more changes, opportunities, and influences. It's not easy. Our job as parents is to seize the God-given opportunity to keep looking for ways to encourage and help them make good decisions, to support them, to teach them, to pray for them, and to help them prioritize all the stuff they're juggling. They will then be better prepared to move through their teenage years into the independence of a God-glorifying adulthood. Parents, our job is to gradually ease our children into taking ownership of their own lives.

15 TEENAGERS NEED PARENTS WHO COMMUNICATE A GOD-HONORING BODY IMAGE PERSPECTIVE.

In today's appearance-oriented world, chances are good that our children won't get the right body-image perspective anywhere else. Of course, gaining the right perspective begins by showering your children with love and acceptance that isn't conditional on what they look like. It continues by carefully watching what we say to them regarding their appearance. Have you ever caught yourself criticizing them about their weight, body shape, or complexion? Those words not only hurt, but they affirm the faulty notion that "I am what I look like." In today's world, these words are especially hurtful. Instead, we should take the time to teach about the inward qualities of a Christ-like life, something that is most powerfully taught through our words and example. Be sure your example includes responsible stewardship and care of your own body. Be sure your example doesn't include an unhealthy obsession with your own appearance. Prayerfully work to develop your own inward character in a God-honoring direction. Your children need to know that while people may emphasize the outward appearance, God is concerned with the development of their hearts (see 1 Samuel 16:7 for God's perspective).

16 IT'S IMPORTANT TO THINK *WITH* YOUR TEENAGERS.

One of the hardest things I've had to learn as a parent of teenagers is to stop my tendency to always want to think *for* my children. I have a tendency to jump in, tell them how it is, issue an instruction or dictate, and then expect them to follow. But I've learned that since my children are in the process of developing their ability to think for themselves, the best thing I can do is to think along *with* them. It's important for us to continue to offer structure, guidance, direction, advice, and explanations, but we also need to give our teenagers the freedom to learn how to make good decisions on their own. If we continue to do all the thinking for our kids, we will be raising adults who have difficulty making ethical, vocational, marital, educational, time management, and a host of other important choices. Here's a little rule to follow: When they're children, we think *for* them. As they move into adolescence, we think *with* them, tempering their decisions by modeling and talking about choices that bring honor and glory to God. We do this so that when they become adults, we will have launched them into a life of being able to competently *think for themselves* in responsible, God-honoring ways.

17 TAKE YOUR TEENAGERS' SHIFTING EMOTIONS SERIOUSLY.

I caved in far too often to the temptation to write off my teenagers' emotions as silly and childish. My insensitivity communicated not only that I didn't care, but that I was rejecting them. What I eventually learned—the hard way!—is that my children's emotional resilience depended greatly on the relationship they had with us as parents. They needed us to hang in there with them and to love them despite the emotional highs and lows over what to us, as adults, seemed like trivial stuff. What may seem like an overreaction to us is in reality them handling their lives in the best way they know how. Our job is to realize that they're not yet adults. They don't have our maturity, but they're on their way. We need to be sensitive and loving if we are going to fulfill our role to lead them to an emotionally stable adulthood.

18 SEE AND CELEBRATE YOUR TEENAGERS' STRENGTHS.

Do you remember your own middle school years? For most of us, it was brutal. Some things never change. Young peers can create, find, and point out all kinds of negative things in ways that are now sometimes defined as "bullying" or "harassment." But if your home is a place of refuge from that craziness, you will be instilling a healthy sense of resiliency that can sustain your children through the pressure. One way to do this is to take the opposite approach of their peers, who are all too quick to point out and celebrate deficiencies. Look for and encourage your teenagers to develop their God-given gifts and abilities. Compliment them on their successes.

19 BEING A GOOD EXAMPLE INCLUDES SHARING YOUR OWN STRUGGLES AND DOUBTS.

The rocky nature of adolescent faith is one of the most heart-breaking and difficult aspects of being a Christian parent who longs to see his children embrace and mature in their own faith. It's frustrating to watch your children take three spiritual steps forward, only to follow that up with four spiritual steps backward. Much of their "wavering" is simply a part of the teenage territory and the process of adopting their family's faith as their own. But maybe an even greater amount of that wavering is rooted in their humanness—a reality that we share with them. Let's face it: We are all sinful and fallen people whose lives, just like the lives of so many biblical characters, are marked by periods of doubt, struggle, problems, and failures.

The Bible is filled with stories of rebellious human beings who were called by God to be his people, but who often stubbornly followed their own will and way. Becoming transparent with our children about the presence of these realities in our own lives can be liberating for them. It not only allows them to see us in our full humanity and dependence on God, but it also gives them permission to struggle, doubt, and sometimes fail. And when we allow them to see us as we are, it encourages them to invite us into their doubts, struggles, problems, and failures. We become credible people to whom they are more likely to turn for guidance, encouragement, and support. Perhaps best of all, they will learn that spiritual maturity is born out of great struggle.

20 SURROUND YOURSELF WITH GOOD AND GOD-HONORING FRIENDS.

It's been said that "It takes a village to raise a child." We've found that to be true. And in our home, the village has included a variety of people including neighbors, coaches, youth workers, grandparents, teachers, and those who attend our church. Our village has also included God-honoring friends who have been present in our children's lives, some of them since our kids were born. Their presence has created relationships that have afforded them great opportunities to speak truth into our children's lives.

Sometimes our children have gone to those people to confide in them or seek advice in times of difficulty. At other times, the relationships have been strong enough for those adult friends to approach our kids to say the difficult things that need to be said, even in times of crisis. Have we been threatened by that? Not at all. Sure, most of what they tell our kids is stuff we've already said over and over again. But sometimes it takes another voice to speak before these things are heard. Take the time to build those friendships, and you can bet you'll be celebrating their positive and Christ-like influence on your children more than once! And if your teenagers clam up and won't talk to you, ask them to talk to one of these other adults they know and trust.

21 GET TO KNOW THEM BY PAYING ATTENTION AND LOOKING AROUND.

When our children hit the teenage years, the nature and content of our conversations with them began to shift. The communication pump had to be primed, and we sometimes felt like we had to pry in order to get them to open up. That's not at all unusual. One of the most helpful ways to continue to listen to your teenagers when they might be talking less is to tune your ears in to some places you might overlook where they "speak" loud and clear. Two of the best ways to listen to the hearts of teenagers in today's world are these: First, "listen" to their bedrooms. Teenage bedrooms are their sanctuaries. You know that because when you walk in, you realize they keep them and decorate them in ways that are much different from your own. Look around at the walls, the floor, and the ceiling. What you'll see is loads of stuff that reflects what they value, what they pay attention to, and what's taking their time. If you see something confusing, ask them about it. Find out what it means to them and why it's important. Second, pay attention to what they're posting in the world of their social media. Frequent visits to your teenagers' Facebook® pages will open your eyes to their interests, circle of friends, hopes, dreams, cares, and concerns. Ask plenty of clarifying questions before drawing conclusions on things that concern you. And once you've listened, take the time to respond in a God-honoring manner with wise direction and advice.

22 SHOOT FOR THE HEART.

Sometimes I've fallen into the trap of believing that if it looks good, it must be good. Then I realize I'm actually an expert in looking good spiritually so those around me believe that I must be good—even when I'm not. We can make the same error in the way we look at and judge our teenagers. We tend to believe that if their outward behavior conforms to the right standards, then everything is fine on the inside. As a result, we sometimes put a premium on outward behavior rather than on inward heart change. Jesus reminds us to shoot for the heart, not the behavior. When speaking to the Pharisees, he refers to the words of Isaiah 29:13. " *'These people honor me with their lips* [outward behavioral conformity], *but their hearts are far from me'* " *(Matthew 15:8).* While it might be easier on us if we demand and receive behavioral conformity from our children, the reality that bears long-term fruit for the kingdom of God is the obedience that flows not from fear, but from a changed heart. In other words, everything that looks all right might not be all right. Our goal should be to raise children who honor Christ with their lips *and* their lives as the obedient outflow from hearts that have been transformed and given new life.

23 LOVE YOUR TEENAGERS.

I know—duh! But then I also know how badly I fail at this most basic of all parenting tasks. Perhaps part of the reason for our failure is our misunderstanding of what love really is. Our culture has drained the word of its meaning to the point where even though it's still one of the most used words, its mention sparks images, thoughts, and ideas that are anything but accurate, and we're left with a deep and harmful misconception of what love is. The place to begin our recovery of an accurate understanding of love is with the God who *is* love and is the author of love. In 1 John

3:11-24, we find that love is something we're commanded to do to each other, something we are to do even when it's not done to us, and something which if missing leads to death. The passage says that love is something Jesus does, that it's costly, and that it's only possible when Jesus lives in and through us. The Greek word used in the Bible for this kind of love is *agape*. Understood correctly, agape is not a feeling but a commitment. It gives of itself without ever expecting anything in return. It is unconditional. It expresses itself fully without reservation, even to those who are unworthy. It loves people even when it doesn't like them or what they are doing. Thanks be to God for Jesus Christ, who loves us unworthy people in this way! And thanks be to God for showing us how to truly love others—including our spouses and children.

24 GET TO KNOW THOSE PEOPLE WHO SERVE YOUR TEENAGERS IN SCHOOL.

Teachers, coaches, club advisers, and administrators are spending six or more hours a day with your teenagers. We've learned to tap into the experience and education of these people. We've tapped into their expertise to learn about how teenagers learn, about adolescent development, and about character formation. In addition, their daily immersion in the world of teenagers gives them great insights into how our culture is changing and the unique issues, problems, challenges, and choices that our children face every day. Finally, we've asked them specific questions about our own children, as spending time with them in the classroom or on the playing field sometimes lets these adults pick up on cares, concerns, and issues we need to be addressing or might be missing. While we certainly don't agree with them on everything, we've come to appreciate the wisdom and expertise of folks who, in the end, equip us to be better and more knowledgeable parents.

25 TAKE AN INTEREST IN THEIR INTERESTS.

This is an easy one if you and your teenager share the same interests. But what happens if you're a left-brained parent raising a right-brained kid? We once heard a parent complain that his son didn't share his love for canoeing. Consequently, he didn't think there'd ever be anything he could do with his son. Sadly, it never crossed the frustrated father's mind that he could enter into his son's world and life by pursuing one of his son's interests. Maybe we should all think about putting some of our own interests aside for a few years so we have more time to pursue the interests of our children *with* our children. Taking an interest in their interests allows us to spend much-needed time with them, opens up opportunities to communicate, builds our relationship, and lets us discover and celebrate our teenagers' gifts and abilities.

DO'S AND DON'TS

26 GROW AS A PARENT BY CONTINUALLY ASKING GOOD QUESTIONS—AND SEEKING ANSWERS.

Even though we were once adolescents ourselves, the cloudy nature of those memories combines with a teenage world that's very different from the one we grew up in to leave us, well, pretty clueless. We need to go out of our way to learn about the uniqueness of living and growing as a teenager in today's world by asking good questions—over and over and over again. Here are some questions to get you started:

- What changes is my child facing as he or she grows from a child into an adult?

- How can I support, love, and lead my teenager through these changes in a way that brings honor and glory to God?

- What must I do to build bridges into my teenager's life to keep the lines of communication open?

- What makes my teenager tick?

- What is my teenager's world like?

- What does my teenager find confusing at this point in his or her life?

- Why does my teenager think and act the way he or she does?

When it comes to our teenagers and their culture, what we don't know, don't want to know, or refuse to know, can hurt them. Ignorance may seem like bliss, but nobody benefits in the end.

27 IF YOU EXPECT PERFECTION, YOU'LL BE DISAPPOINTED.

Because I study youth culture, there's one question I've been asked more than any other: "What's the greatest challenge facing teenagers in today's world?" The answer is easy: Sin. In Genesis 3:6 we read that everything God made and declared as "good" came undone, including people, through the rebellion of humanity. I am a sinner. My children are sinners. All of us are in need of fixing that we can't do for ourselves. We are all in desperate need of redemption through Jesus Christ. While we must never use the reality of human depravity as an excuse for bad behavior or to not pursue spiritual growth, we must never forget that we're all imperfect, flawed people who are in desperate need of a Savior. Don't expect perfection from yourself, your children, or your family. It's bad theology, and it will burden and destroy every member of your family.

 ## DON'T TAKE IT PERSONALLY.

There will be times when your children will criticize, mock, and even reject your best efforts, advice, attempts to connect, or anything else you might do to make them happy. When that happens, move on. Don't base your mood, self-worth, or understanding of your parenting skills and effectiveness on how your kids feel about you or treat you. These words from the writer of Proverbs deserve our attention at times like these: *Trust in the Lord with all your heart; do not depend on your own understanding. Seek his will in all you do, and he will show you which path to take (Proverbs 3:5-6).* Your role is to consistently love and encourage your children while looking to Christ as your rock, along with faithfully and obediently finding your own identity in him and him alone.

IF YOU'RE SUSPICIOUS ABOUT YOUR TEENAGER'S MOODS, DON'T BE AFRAID TO ASK QUESTIONS.

The incidence of depression among children and teenagers is alarmingly high. None of our kids are immune. If we fall into the trap of blaming all of our teenager's negative moodiness on "being a teenager," we run the risk of missing signs of more severe and lasting issues and or problems that could be signs of depression. Don't be timid. If you have suspicions that your child is depressed, ask probing questions in a loving manner. If your suspicions linger or are confirmed, immediately seek the help of a competent Christian counselor.

ASSUME A GOOD "PARENTING POSTURE."

I sometimes think there are only three basic postures we can assume as we approach the task of parenting teenagers. The first posture is what I call the "unrealistic optimist." This is the parent who ho-hums over the teen years, assuming that adolescence is a short-lived life stage that may be filled with ups and downs but is better left alone. Why? Because teenagers will weather it and emerge from it OK. Believing that, the unrealistic optimist takes a hands-off approach, letting nature take its course. The second posture is what I call the "alarmist pessimist." This is the parent who demonizes the teenage years and adolescent culture. Believing there's nothing good or redeemable about adolescence or youth culture, this parent shields their teenagers from the many wonderful things they could and should be experiencing and learning during the teenage years. This parent believes that this is the best way to prepare his or her children for life. While there are certainly times to be optimistic or guarded, embracing these extremes either forfeits our parental responsibility to nurture children in the faith or exasperates them away from faith. Here's a better posture option: "biblical realism." It's a posture that looks realistically at life, parenting, and adolescence through the eyes of God's Word. It's a posture that's not only balanced but also allows us to recognize and address both the good and the bad aspects of everything our teenagers will face in the world.

31 DON'T BE AFRAID TO SAY NO; YOU'RE THEIR PARENT, NOT THEIR FRIEND.

Why do so many parents tiptoe gingerly around their children in today's world? More and more parents are afraid to step up, take the reins, and rule the roost. Instead, parents have become like butlers, available to wait on and serve their kids' every fleeting desire and whim. Fearing rejection, we sometimes go against our better judgment and say yes when we should be saying no. God established the family with a pecking order. Those who are older and wiser (the parents) are charged with the duty of raising, nurturing, and protecting those who are younger and not-so-experienced or wise (the children). Sometimes the very things we need to protect our teenagers from are themselves, their impulsivity, and their lack of good judgment. You have a God-given right *and* responsibility to love your teenager—and to sometimes step in and say no.

32 YOUR TEENAGER IS NOT YOUR "DO OVER."

We were once at a high school football game where a father in the stands spent his time screaming and yelling at his son out on the field. About halfway through the game, another man in the stands turned around, looked up at his screaming friend, and said, "Hey, Bill, you'd think that was you out there on that field!" It took a split second for Bill to heartily yell back his answer: "It is!" Too bad for Bill's poor son. Bill should have named his son "Mulligan." In today's achievement-oriented and status-conscious world, we can allow ourselves to feel like we don't measure up now, nor did we measure up when we were teenagers.

Hoping to improve our own status and somehow redeem the perceived failures and get over the regrets of our adolescent years, we attempt to relive our lives through our children. We pressure them into activities that they don't want to be involved in, fostering resentment. Or we spend loads of time and money on activities that they love, fostering entitlement. Both are wrong.

33 HELP THEM LEARN FROM THEIR FAILURES.

Remember flunking a test? getting cut from a team? getting caught drinking? losing your virginity? wrecking the family car? having to attend summer school? Remember hating those moments—feeling like your life was crashing down quickly—and desperately wanting to snap your fingers to work some magic to get out of there? Chances are you now look back on those times of failure as watershed moments; times in your life where you learned great lessons, where God helped you make a directional adjustment that had a positive impact on your life, where you learned more about your God-given gifts and abilities, and where you learned great lessons in handling hardship. Your teenagers are going to fail and feel like failures at some point (or points) during their adolescent years. Walk through those failures with them by listening to their pain, processing their pain with them, sharing stories of how you learned from your own failures, and offering an eternal perspective on how God grows us through our failures.

34 LET THEM PUT OUT THEIR OWN FIRES.

I recently heard the term "trophy kids" used to describe teenagers and young adults who grew up in homes where their parents were more like maids and butlers than moms and dads. If you've been around those privileged and entitled individuals, you know just how destructive that kind of parenting can be. Many of them grow up unable to handle responsibility or live responsibly because they were never given any responsibilities. Everything was done for them. Then there are those teenagers who made messes but never had to clean them up. Dad and Mom would step in to soften the blow of consequences or even make excuses in an effort to get their kids off the hook. Always running interference for your children and bailing them out so they don't have to suffer the consequences of their actions does deep and lasting harm. When your teenagers make a mess of things accidentally or deliberately, walk with them as they suffer the disciplinary consequences for their actions. Let them pay their traffic tickets, serve their detentions, and issue the necessary apologies.

35 WHEN YOU'RE WRONG, ADMIT IT.

Notice this thought is not, "*If* you're wrong, admit it." We all have times when we speak too soon, respond inappropriately, overreact, yell, embarrass, and just plain mess up in ways too numerous to count. When that happens, we can't walk away without making an apology to our children and asking for their forgiveness. While our wrong actions set a horrible example, righting that wrong is the right thing to do, and it provides a powerful example of the redemptive process. It's been said there are three things you'll never hear a man say: "I'm lost," "I can't fix it," and "I was wrong." Let's make sure our children hear us say, "I'm sorry."

36 RAISE CHILDREN, NOT GRASS.

There's an old story about a man who got his neighbors angry when he stopped maintaining his once lush lawn. When the man and his wife were newlyweds, they moved into their house, and he painstakingly worked on the landscaping. But when they started having children, less time was spent on the lawn. Weeds overtook the grass. Bare spots began to appear where his growing children would play their regular kickball games with the other neighborhood children. One day his next door neighbor asked, "When are you going to take care of that lawn of yours?" The active and involved father quickly replied, "I'm raising kids, not grass." We only have 1,440 minutes in each day. We choose to spend each minute doing something somewhere. During the few fast and furious years you have your children in the house, why not carefully invest as many of those minutes as possible in them, rather than in things like long overtime hours at work, playing golf, or any time-consuming pursuits? They can easily steal away the time you could be pouring into your children.

37 DON'T ASSUME THAT OTHER PARENTS THINK THE WAY YOU DO.

When our children were young, we became involved in a circle of friends in our community who shared time with us sitting together on the sidelines, at school functions, and in our daily comings and goings. Those relationships continued until our children graduated from high school. We made the mistake of assuming that just because they were our friends, we shared the same parenting values and standards. There were many matters on which we were in agreement. So imagine our surprise when we would learn that some of these friends were more than happy to break the law by opening their homes as safe places for teenagers to gather and drink, host coed sleepovers, or fail to provide supervision. Before your children spend time at other people's homes, pick up the phone and make a call to ask questions regarding what is and is not allowed to happen at those homes, along with who will be present to supervise. Then, based on that knowledge, make decisions on where and where not your own kids are allowed to go. Protecting your children from harm and providing for their well-being might not make you popular, but it is the right thing to do.

BE READY AND WILLING TO DROP EVERYTHING.

Let your teenagers know that there's nothing you aren't willing to put on hold if they need you. Of course, you want them to learn how to be polite, to not interrupt, and to discern those things that are of urgent importance from those that aren't. But you want your children to know that if they are in trouble or in need, you will drop what you're doing—no matter what that is—to be at their side to offer guidance, advice, love, help, and support. Be ready to open the door to your office, to pick up the phone, to leave work, or to cancel a trip when the responsibilities of parenting warrant it.

39 BE SURE YOUR FAMILY IS ALL IT WAS MEANT TO BE.

From the beginning of time, God made the family to be a special place for children. It's the place they are to be born into, loved, nurtured, and led to a spiritually, emotionally, and physically healthy adulthood. Children need a mother and father who love God, love each other, and love the kids. Anything less and the family fails to exist and function as it was meant to. Do everything in your power to build your faith, your marriage, and your relationship with your children. But if your marriage and family have already been broken by choice or circumstance, don't throw up your hands in failure. God can still redeem your situation. Surround yourself and your children with the support system of a church family that understands and will minister to your unique situation.

40 SPEND TIME WITH YOUR TEENAGERS.

Don't believe the lie that "quality time" is just as important as "quantity time." In reality, the two go hand in hand. Don't invoke the myth of quality time to justify your absence from home to pursue career success and your personal interests and goals. When high school students were asked about their wishes for a better life, you might be surprised at what they said. A small number wished for more money and a bigger house—not surprising since those things are terribly overvalued in our culture. But here's the thing those high schoolers wished for more than anything else: "More time spent with my family." Guess what? You can make that wish come true.

CULTURE

41 THE WORLD OF YOUTH CULTURE SHAPES KIDS IN POWERFUL WAYS.

Every day, marketers and media makers drop a new load of stuff into the world of your teenagers. Because your children are growing through change-filled adolescent years that leave them questioning anything and everything about life, they're incredibly vulnerable to this stuff's ability to serve as a map, shaping their values, attitudes, and behaviors. As a result, growing up has become even more difficult and confusing. There are new problems, pressures, choices, challenges, and expectations that are more complex than ever before. It's a different world from the world we grew up in. To help your teenagers navigate their way through this rapidly changing youth culture according to God's map, you need to work hard to keep abreast of these rapid changes. If you don't, the cultural and generational gap that exists between you and your teenagers will only grow, making it difficult to effectively communicate, love, and parent. Keep your eyes and ears open so you can stay culturally informed. (We can help you do that at the Center for Parent/Youth Understanding; visit cpyu.org for daily updates on today's youth culture.)

42 WRONG INFLUENCES CAN EMERGE ANYWHERE, ANYTIME.

It doesn't matter where you live, where you go to church, or where you send your teenager to school. Every teenager can and will be influenced by the culture—the good *and* the bad—and it can happen anywhere at any time. No church, school, family, or teenager is immune. And when we fail to see the influence culture *is* having, we wind up losing the influence we *should be* having. Because we want to help our children navigate through the influences, we should know the influences so we can discuss them with our kids. When it comes to teenagers and their culture, what we don't know—or don't want to know or refuse to know—*can* hurt them.

43 READ WHAT THEY READ, WATCH WHAT THEY WATCH, AND LISTEN TO WHAT THEY LISTEN TO.

Sounds a bit scary—and it might be. But it's necessary work if you want to raise teenagers who can navigate the complexities of life in today's world and for the rest of their lives. By observing and questioning your children, you can quickly learn which specific cultural voices are speaking loud and clear into their lives. Then taking time to interact with those voices firsthand helps you to understand and relate to your children while equipping them to relate to the world around them, which is exactly what Jesus wants them to do. This helps us to raise teenagers who are wise enough to filter these voices in a way that allows them to discern the good from the bad. Don't think that observing and learning about youth culture implies participation in or acceptance of all aspects of that youth culture. It simply means that you're taking the time to know as much as you can about your children and their influential world, a necessary step toward equipping them to live as lights in the midst of darkness.

44 TALK WITH YOUR TEENAGERS ABOUT POP CULTURE SPIRITUALITY.

Your teenager's culture is filled with spiritual themes, spiritual questions, spiritual beliefs, and various concepts of God. This shouldn't be surprising as all human beings are on a quest to discover meaning and purpose in life. Sadly, pop culture rarely promotes a spirituality that is consistently biblical. Our children are being encouraged to step up to the "spiritual buffet line" where they fill their plates according to what they think they're hungry for at that moment. At a time when your teenagers are forming the spiritual values and beliefs they'll embrace for life, popular culture encourages them to forget Christianity and the God of the Bible to pursue whatever combination of religious beliefs makes sense to them, based on their own personal preferences. While the messages the culture promotes are discouraging, our teenagers' spiritual self-awareness should be encouraging. The culture encourages them to ask significant questions and to seek answers. This gives us a great opportunity to provide biblical answers. Stand over your teenager's shoulder to look and listen for references to God and spirituality that are present in the world. Filter what you see and hear through God's Word and then patiently and diligently continue to point out the truth and challenge the errors. You'll be helping them to develop the ability to discern that which is true, good, and right from that which is anything but biblical.

45 IT'S ALL RELATIVE—BUT IT SHOULDN'T BE.

Here's a little phrase you may have heard from your teenager in one form or another in response to your efforts to provide parental guidance and direction: "That may be OK for you. But it's not right for me." Welcome to the emerging world of moral relativism. Your teenagers have been encouraged—not by you, we hope—to create truth for themselves. In their world, the only rule is this: There are no rules. There is no universal standard of right and wrong. Rather, it's up to the individual to determine what is right and what works for him or her. Take a look around and you'll see evidence of teenagers living under the authority of self as they make all kinds of lifestyle choices. The end result of the loss of this shared moral compass is anarchy. Taken to an extreme, your children won't be choosing to obey you. They'll just be, well, choosing. While it makes our parenting task that much harder, we must confront moral relativism whenever it rears its ugly head in our children's lives. Always be ready to lovingly and gracefully point out the contrast between God's never-changing standards and the fluid, ever-changing personal "truths" of moral relativism.

46 ENCOURAGE COMPASSION OVER COMPETITION.

Think about the familiar parable of the good Samaritan. Jesus told that story so his followers would know they should view anyone in need as a neighbor. He told about a Samaritan who gave everything in response to a wounded man's need, and then instructed us to "go and do the same." But here's the rub for those of us who live in today's world, including our teenagers: The message our culture encourages us to believe and follow is the exact opposite. Instead of looking out for others, we're to look out for number one. In this kind of world, generosity decreases while selfishness increases. In this kind of world, civility declines. In this kind of world, our teenagers are encouraged to do anything and everything possible to get ahead of anyone and everyone else. As Christian parents who long for our children to follow Christ, we not only need to go against the flow of this selfish way of thinking and living, but we also need to help our kids do the same. How? Carefully monitor your lifestyle, limit your consumption, increase your giving, get involved in social justice issues, and encourage your children to do the same. We need to raise compassionate—rather than competitive—teenagers.

47 SEX EDUCATION— DESPERATELY NEEDED.

"When should I talk to my kids about sex?" Another question I hear all the time. Usually, the parent asking the question is hoping for an answer on the higher end of the number scale— like "when they turn 18." Not a good idea in a world that says to children and teenagers of all ages, "When it comes to your sexuality, go ahead and do *whatever* you want, with *whomever* you want, *wherever* you want, *whenever* you want, and *however* you want." This "the choice is yours" way of looking at sexuality is not what they need to hear, but it is what they're hearing. The sex education our children do so desperately need is one that leads them to understand that God created sex to be wonderful and fulfilling when experienced within the bounds of his plan. So who's going to tell them? God's given you the responsibility to nurture them in the faith as it relates to all of life. And the good news is that research points to the fact that children want to learn about sexuality from their parents, not from the TV or on the playground! Take time to know God's design, to model God's design, and to talk with them about God's design in an age-appropriate manner.

GIVE YOUR TEENAGERS THE BEST LIFE, NOT THE GOOD LIFE.

If we relentlessly pursue the American Dream and the desire to pass the material benefits of the good life on to our children, bad things happen. Experts who work with children who have been given too much by their parents have developed diagnoses known as "Affluenza" and "Rich Kids Syndrome." Its victims aren't just from wealthy homes. The disease is as common in middle-class and lower-class homes as it is in homes with lots of money. The danger rests in the fact that we are fostering and encouraging idolatry. What's the alternative to giving our children the good life? It's giving them the best life. Our lives and actions should communicate to our children that the best life is found by living in relationship with God, living out his will, and by pursuing his standards of success. The best life consists of directing all we have, all we do, and all we are toward loving and serving God in every nook, cranny, and minute of our lives. The "best life" includes the ability to tell the difference between "needs" and "wants." And then, because of our love for God, we should love those around us rather than treating them as competition or means to material ends. The best life comes in the pursuit of Mark 12:29-31.

49 MOTH AND RUST, MOTH AND RUST.

In our house, we temper our discouragement over stuff that breaks by reminding each other that in this world, stuff rots. You'll often hear us admonish one another with the simple little phrase, "Moth and rust, moth and rust." It's a healthy reminder when you've been raised and nurtured by a consumer-oriented and market-driven society to have the latest, greatest, and best new item. It's a verbal reality check that gives us perspective. Jesus spent quite a bit of time challenging this age-old tendency toward materialistic idolatry. He said, *"Don't store up treasures here on earth, where moths eat them and rust destroys them, and where thieves break in and steal. Store your treasures in heaven, where moths and rust cannot destroy, and thieves do not break in and steal" (Matthew 6:19-20).* We need to teach our children—and ourselves—that the only treasures that matter are heavenly ones. Possessions mean nothing. If you're not pounding that life-saving truthful message home, chances are your teenagers might not hear it anywhere else.

50 EASE UP ON THE SPORTS PRESSURE.

Researchers at Michigan State University report that 70 percent of people who play youth sports drop out of them by the age of 13.

The reason? Too much pressure from parents and a society that puts a premium on athletic ability, performance, and winning. Sadly, many of these dropouts are gifted athletes who should be developing their God-given athletic gifts and abilities long into the teen years. Others are late bloomers whose discouragement leads them to hang it up, causing them to miss out on the years of successful play that could be theirs if they would only be encouraged to hang in there long enough for their bodies and skills to develop. Then there are those who continue on while allowing the pressure to excel to lead them to try to get an edge through cheating and performance-enhancing drugs. The youth sports landscape is not good. Want to know how bad it's become? Go to a local soccer field where elementary-aged kids are playing an organized game. Don't watch what's happening on the field. Turn sideways and look down the sideline. Just keep on looking and listening. What you see and hear might break your heart. Then ask yourself, "Am I putting too much pressure on my children?" Make sure your expectations are reasonable.

51 MEDIA PLAYS A HUGE ROLE IN TEENAGERS' LIVES.

The latest research says that the average 8- to 18-year-old is spending 7 hours and 38 minutes a day using media of some kind. Much of that time is spent using multiple media platforms simultaneously! To fully understand the powerful role media play in their lives, we must remember that teenagers are in a tumultuous period of change. They also want to know what life is all about and how to live in the world. Maybe the best way to say it is, they're sponges! Our media meet them where they are and answer their questions, provide guidance for life, and tell them what to value and how to live in the world. Media serve as a map. But isn't that our job as parents? In addition to helping our teenagers map out their lives, we need to study the map of their media. Then we can point out to them when media are sending them in the right direction leading them down very dangerous paths.

52 SET MEDIA LIMITS.

Remember, the more media a teenager watches and consumes, the more those media can subtly persuade—just like the slow yet steady shaping "influence" a stream has on a pebble. Physicians even recognize this fact—so much so, that they are now encouraging parents to set limits in terms of how much time children use media, and the type of media they consume. Pediatricians are now warning parents that early and frequent media use and overuse contributes to a host of health problems, including obesity, violent/aggressive behavior, tobacco and alcohol use, and early sexual activity. As Christian parents, we should be concerned about the fallout on their spiritual development, their beliefs, and the resulting behaviors. In addition, media time cuts into family time, hindering face-to-face communication. All that is good reason for us to set media time and content limits for our children.

53 EXPOSE MEDIA'S LIES.

Here's a statement you won't find the least bit surprising: Media often tell lies. When our teenagers haven't learned how to view the world through the lens of God's Word, they risk believing and living the media's destructive lies rather than believing and living God's life-giving and liberating truth. Not only that, but it makes it more difficult for us to lead our children into an understanding of God's will and way when they've been numbed to the truth. When messages from media—particularly entertainment media—stand in opposition to God's truth, our teenagers are faced with a dilemma that leaves them wondering, "Who and what should I believe?" It's our parental responsibility to spot the media's lies, teach our kids to spot the lies, and then to answer them with the truth. For example, media messages leave them believing that to be worthwhile, you must be beautiful. But God says, "I care about *who* you are, not what you look like." Media messages tell them to avoid pain and pursue pleasure at all costs. Jesus tells his followers to expect suffering and exercise perseverance. Expose the lies, and proclaim the truth.

54
LET YOUR TEENAGERS KNOW THAT THEY'RE MORE THAN JUST A "THING."

There's a big difference between seeing yourself as a meaningless object or a human being instilled with dignity. Sadly, the world of advertising is pounding our teenagers with a nonstop deluge of images that support a self-understanding that's more like the former than the latter. Our children are being taught to objectify others and to be objectified themselves. For a long time, females have been portrayed as "eye candy" and "boy toys." They've learned that their value and worth has been based on what they look like and how they serve the needs of others as sexual things. Now the pressure's being felt by our boys as well. When you get hammered with these messages from birth, they're bound to stick. You should be committed to helping your teenager not only identify marketing stereotypes, but to consciously and thoughtfully process them out loud in a way that leads them to realize how far these images stray from God's order and design.

55
KEEP THE BEDROOM UNPLUGGED.

According to the latest research, more than 70 percent of 8- to 18-year-olds have a television in their bedroom. Most of those

TVs have a seemingly limitless number of channel options being funneled in through cable or satellites. And you know what happens? Teenagers go to the privacy of their own rooms to watch television, while other family members retreat to their bedrooms for their private viewing experiences. Nobody is watching together. Consequently, nobody is filtering what's appropriate and inappropriate viewing content. So teenagers who are allowed to watch anything and everything don't have any adults present to help them process what they're seeing and hearing. Limit the number of media outlets in their bedrooms. Don't allow your children to have a television and online access in their bedroom. Too much media opportunity typically leads to too much media time, unsupervised media time, and less time together as a family.

56 CREATE MOMENTS WITHOUT NOISE.

Activities and noise, activities and noise, activities and noise. That's the rhythm of most children's lives. We've heard countless parents and youth workers lament the fact that teenagers' lives are so noisy these days that when it all stops and they find themselves in the midst of silence, they don't know what to do. When they lose the ability to enjoy the silence, they lose the ability to listen to and communicate with God, to sit quietly and think, and to simply find moments of solace in the midst of a busy day. Do what you can to make your home a place that's "unplugged" for long segments of time. It will encourage your children to slow down and relax, and it will foster the much-needed discipline of taking time to simply rest in the quiet.

SPIRITUAL NURTURE

 WANT TO KNOW WHAT YOUR TEENAGER *REALLY* WANTS? GOD.

Like you, me, and every other human being who's walked the face of the earth, your teenager was made by God for a relationship *with* God. Because our rebellion and sin severed that relationship, we are left with a deep and gnawing desire to have that relationship restored. Whether he or she knows it or not, your teenager wants more than anything else to have the God-shaped hole in his or her soul filled by the Creator. A teenager's deepest hunger is for heaven. If you listen hard, you will hear him or her asking questions about how to get home. Let this fact spur you on to consciously and constantly point your teenager to the cross of Jesus Christ and our true home.

DON'T PULL YOUR CHILDREN OUT OF THE WORLD.

Some of us in the church believe that we're doing a good job if we're raising our children like those three little monkeys: Hear No Evil, Speak No Evil, See No Evil. We believe that if we can somehow shield teenagers from the evil influences of the world, then evil won't be a part of their lives. Bad and wrong idea. When Jesus calls his followers (including our teenagers) to be salt and light in the world, he is calling us (as he prayed in John 17) to be *in* but not *of* the world. Going deep in the things of God and nurturing our teenagers into that same deep place is a way of embracing the balanced lifestyle that one of my heroes of the faith, John Stott, describes as being "spiritually distinct, but not socially segregated." One of the marks of spiritual maturity is endeavoring to maintain a redemptive presence in the world. That is, after all, the will of our heavenly Father.

YOU CAN'T DRAG YOUR CHILDREN KICKING AND SCREAMING INTO GOD'S KINGDOM.

Only God's Spirit is able to draw people to himself. We can't force our teenagers into following Jesus or strong-arm them into the kingdom of God. But we can and must strive to be faithful and obedient followers of Jesus ourselves. Our children have been given minds of their own. Pray for your teenagers to come to a saving faith in Jesus Christ. Model and talk about what it means to follow Jesus. Trust God to work out his plan in his time and his way with your children.

60 FEELINGS VS. TRUTH—TEACH THEM WHICH SHOULD WIN.

If they would be honest with us, our teenagers would tell us that "It just felt right" or "I felt like it" serves far too often as their guide for life. Not surprisingly, today's culture encourages that kind of feeling-driven living. What a shame it would be if history remembered our generation of Christian parents as people who didn't do anything to help their children choose to listen to God instead of their windblown emotions. Feelings should never eclipse God's truth. We must walk our teenagers through the Scriptures to show them examples of people who allowed their emotions to eclipse the truth—and then suffered the consequences (including David with Bathsheba, Lot's wife, Ananias and Sapphira). We must walk them through the stories of our own lives by sharing the good, the bad, and the ugly regarding the feelings-based and truth-based choices we've made.

61

ALLOW YOUR TEENAGERS ROOM TO QUESTION GOD AND MAKE THEIR FAITH THEIR OWN.

We live in a world where terms like "pluralism" and "tolerance" have created an environment where teenagers are encouraged to try on different faith systems (after all, they're all the same aren't they?) or even create their own by picking bits and pieces from the spiritual buffet table based on their personal tastes and preferences. No doubt, we should counter these dangerous practices by pointing our teenagers to the truth. But while we're pointing them to the truth, we must realize that they *will* be curious about other faith systems, they *will* question Christianity, and they *will* experience deep doubt and might even wander. When this happens, remain faithful and trust God to do his work in your teenagers. What could in fact be happening is that God is taking your teenagers on a journey to a vital relationship with Jesus Christ through a sometimes long process that includes periods of doubt, questioning, examination, and speculation. Pray hard. Love them. Never stop speaking the truth. And most of all, trust in God's sovereignty as he works out his plan for your teenagers in his way and in his time.

62   REAL SPIRITUAL GROWTH IS A TIME-CONSUMING PROCESS.

If you're a Christian parent who is growing in your faith, your current level of spiritual maturity and understanding isn't the same as it was when you were a teenager. You've gone through a process of spiritual growth that isn't yet complete. So why do we get so stuck on expecting our teenagers to be at the same place we are? Like us, they're still in process and they need time to grow. Here's the danger that comes with heaping unrealistic expectations on our children to be at a place of full and faithful Christian maturity: We may actually be encouraging them to conform to outward standards of behavior and conduct that they adopt simply to appease us and—let's be honest—get us off their backs! We need to be patient as God's Spirit changes their hearts. Our desire should be for changed hearts that, in turn, lead to changed lifestyles. Outward conformity looks nice and can make us look good as parents, but it's only a ruse that will someday be exposed.

63   YOU ARE A PROPHET.

The Bible tells us about the way things in our world should be. As Christian parents raising teenagers trying to find their way through a world that's broken and terribly mixed up, we are given a responsibility to help them wade through the muck by leading them into an understanding of the way things *should be*. In Old Testament times, God raised up prophets who were called to do just that. In today's world, God has given parents that responsibility in our children's lives. But how are we to speak prophetically? In the Sermon on the Mount, Jesus gives a great example. He used "You have heard...but I say" statements. Jesus used this simple little formula to issue correctives to the faulty cultural messages people had heard, believed, and followed. Jesus confronted and exposed the cultural "You have heard" statements with his Word-centered "I say" declarations. We need to follow his example. When you discover a cultural lie that your teenagers are facing or embracing, shed the light of God's life-giving truth on that lie. A hallmark of God-honoring parenting is continually assuming the prophetic posture, helping our children see the difference between the ways of the world ("you have heard") and the ways of living according to God's kingdom priorities ("but Jesus says").

64 LIVE THE TRUTH.

Perhaps you've used these words as a parent: "Do as I say, not as I do." Teenagers are sharp—very sharp. It doesn't take them long to know what we truly believe based on their observations of how we behave. The *who* you are sends strong messages about the *who* they've been made to be. Actions *do* speak louder than words. But don't just live the truth because you know your teenagers are watching. Live the truth out of a heart that is truly pursuing God. That's what your children need to see. When loving and serving God becomes the central overriding passion and purpose in our lives, teaching the truths of God's Word to our children will be much, much easier.

PRAY FOR THE KINGDOM TO COME IN YOUR TEENAGERS' LIVES.

Most of us have memorized the Lord's Prayer at some point in our lives. In our church, we recite that prayer each week in worship. Think about the part where we ask the Lord to let his kingdom to come and for his will to be done on earth as it is in heaven. Have you ever thought about praying that prayer and asking God to send his kingdom—his will, his way, his order, his priorities, his way of living—into the lives of your teenagers? That's the kind of living they were made for. That's the kind of living we need to hope for. It might sound a bit strange, but when our teenagers have been resistant to living under God's kingdom reign, we've prayed that they would be unsettled and even miserable until they choose to walk in his will and way again.

PRAY THAT YOUR TEENAGERS' CORRUPTION WOULD REAR ITS UGLY HEAD NOW, RATHER THAN LATER.

OK, this is a strange thought, especially when we hope for a safe, smooth, and problem-free ride through the years of adolescence with our teenagers. Why in the world would we ever hope for difficulty?!? Well, here's the deal: We need to constantly remind ourselves that part of our teenagers' makeup (because they are human) is that just like us, they were born with a tendency to sin. In other words, they didn't have to be taught how to do wrong. The Apostle Paul recognizes this reality when he instructs parents to teach their children how to do right by bringing them up *with the discipline and instruction that comes from the Lord (Ephesians 6:4).* But in many Christian homes, teenagers will often hide their sinful natures through behavioral conformity that doesn't reflect the true condition of their hearts. But if the symptoms of their corrupt nature come out when they are young, we have the opportunity to address those heart matters now. If those things are left to rear their ugly heads later in life and our adult children don't recognize or know how to deal with them, think about the great troubles and difficulties that will create. Pray that God would reveal your teenagers' sin issues and tendencies now so that you are able to teach them how to recognize and deal with them now—and for the rest of their lives. When God answers this prayer, it's certainly not easy. But it's important to face and address their sin tendencies now so you can nurture your teenagers' hearts into a God-honoring adulthood, rather than having to face them later.

67 ENCOURAGE MISSIONS AND SERVICE.

Discourage a spirit of self-centered materialism while encouraging a lifestyle of obedience to Christ by getting involved *with* your children in missions and service. One of the marks of today's generation of teenagers is a greater willingness to make a difference. This is a good sign and an opportunity we can't let slip through the cracks. By modeling and encouraging selfless involvement in missions and service, you can grow a desire in your children to serve others in the name of Jesus Christ. Enable them to participate with their peers. In addition, take the opportunity to serve with them. We've learned that enabling our teenagers to go on mission trips and going with them ourselves has been a great way for them to grow in their faith and in their relationship with us.

68 YOU'RE A SIGNPOST; IN WHAT DIRECTION ARE YOU POINTING?

It's easy for teenagers to get lost in the negative aspects of today's culture. They're standing at the crossroads, deciding which way to go. The options are many, the signposts are eye-catching, and the directions they point can be dangerous. As their parents, we have to keep our eyes on them. We need to be right where they are. We must be aware of the signposts they are following. And we should serve as signposts to point them in the right way. In his classic book on discipleship, *The Fight*, Dr. John White reminds us of our need to become signposts. White writes, "A signpost points to a destination. It matters little whether the signpost is pretty or ugly, old or new. It helps if the lettering is bold and clear. But the essential features are that it must point in the right direction and be clear about what it is pointing to." Will we serve as signposts for truth, pointing down the narrow path that leads to life—signposts so big and convincing that we eclipse the many signposts already there?

69 ENCOURAGE THEM TO PURSUE FELLOWSHIP WITH THE LARGER AND DIVERSE BODY OF CHRIST.

I'm convinced that one of the reasons so many teenagers and young adults are walking away from the heritage of their faith is that we haven't given them a complete heritage. Many of our teenagers have a church experience that's filled with nothing but worship, classes, youth group, and activities with peers of the same age. They haven't worshipped intergenerationally, with people of all ages. Nor have they been in social situations with the older members of the church. What happens is that we "socialize" them into thinking that anything related to their faith is only relevant when experienced with people of like age. We rob them of those opportunities to experience life in the larger body of Christ—opportunities that allow them to benefit from the full breadth of gifts, ages, wisdom, experience, and abilities of the people that make up the church. Our teenagers' spiritual maturity is best fed, grown, and cemented into maturity when fellowship is broad-based rather than with just their peers.

GROWING UP/
ADOLESCENT
DEVELOPMENT

70 YOUR KIDS ARE GROWING UP.

I once heard someone say that he was happily holding his newborn daughter—and then he blinked. When he opened his eyes, she was heading off to college. Then we had four kids of our own—and it happened to us. Your teenagers are on a rapid path from the dependence of childhood (yep, relying on you for everything) to the independence of adulthood. On the way, they will pass through the years of unprecedented change, confusion, and questioning that we call adolescence. God gave your children to you to steward by preparing them for life on their own. You may be consciously or unconsciously tempted to try to keep them from growing up. But doing so will only hurt them in the end. Sadly, more and more young adults are living in an extended adolescence—and still living at home!—fed and fueled by doting parents. Don't make that mistake. Your job is to prepare them to live as faithful, obedient, and God-honoring *independent* adults. The goal of adolescence is independence.

71 THEY'RE GETTING AND LOOKING OLDER—YOUNGER!

God made your children to grow up. The physical metamorphosis from child to adult begins (and happens pretty fast!) as their bodies produce and secrete hormones that lead to the onset of puberty. In case you haven't noticed, today's kids are hitting puberty at an earlier age. Did you know that back in the 19th century the average age for the onset of puberty was 17? Now, it's 12! Most kids experience puberty between the ages of 11 and 14, but it can occur anytime between the ages of 10 and 17. After I finally gave up on my quest to find a pause button for my children, I realized God had ordained when each of my kids would start the process. When I finally had that figured out, I quickly realized that God has also given me the responsibility to understand what changes my sons and daughters would face and to assume my role as a parent to guide them through it. And remember, just because they look older doesn't mean they are older. Keep that in mind in order to avoid having unrealistic expectations for your teenagers.

72 THE TEENAGE BRAIN IS A FUNNY THING.

When God made our bodies, he made them incredibly complex. Recent developments in the area of brain research are especially eye-opening for parents of teenagers. In the very recent past, it was believed that the human brain was fully formed sometime between the ages of 8 and 12. But the technology that allows us to see into the brain is now showing that the brain is an organ that grows and transitions over time—just like everything else about our teenagers. Now we know that the brain isn't fully formed until the age of 24 or 25 and that the prefrontal cortex (the part of the brain that controls impulses, planning, organizing, prioritizing, judging consequences, and self-control) is the last part to develop. That might explain a few things!

73 LIVING WITH A MOODY TEENAGER? YOU'RE NOT ALONE.

Because of all the changes and pressures teenagers face, mood swings from the highest of elated highs to the lowest of depressing lows can occur suddenly—and end just as quickly. Some of these mood swings are directly related to the physical changes taking place in their bodies. Or they can be related to the social pressures teenagers face, including the desire to fit in, the volatile nature of teenage relationships, and the joys and sorrows related to young teenage "love." The bottom line in regards to teenage emotions is this: Strange behavior is often normal. Remember how moody you were at that age? While you might be tempted to lock them (or yourself) up in a closet until these years pass, you can't forget that you play an important role in helping your teenagers understand and handle their emotions in God-honoring ways. They are looking to you for guidance, direction, and safe harbor.

74 IDENTITY—THAT'S WHAT THEY'RE SEEKING TO DISCOVER.

The stereotype of teenagers back in the hippie days of the 1960s depicted them talking about trying to "find themselves." While today's teenagers rarely hitchhike to California as part of that quest, the single most important developmental issue in a teenager's life is still *identity formation*. In the end, every teenager chooses to find his or her identity in something. The place they land now in terms of understanding themselves will determine what they believe and who they are for the rest of their lives. That's why one of the most important parenting issues we face is the identity formation of our teenagers. In a perfect world, our children would answer the question Who am I? by finding their identity in who they are as unique individuals created by God in the image of God for a relationship with him. But our fallen world gives our children countless other options. Consequently, they embrace idolatry when they find their identity, value, and worth in something or someone other than God. In today's world, our teenagers are prone to walk the dangerous path of seeking identity in sexual partners, romantic interests, academic accomplishments, athletic achievements, money, possessions, pleasurable experiences, peer approval, or even the pursuit of noble social causes. To help your teenagers navigate through these options and into the place where they find their identity in Jesus Christ alone, openly recognize and discuss these dangerous options with your children. And remember this: Where you have found your identity speaks louder than any words you can muster.

THE FUTURE IS THE GREAT UNKNOWN THEY THINK ABOUT NOW.

When he was little, our son Josh informed us that he was going to be just like Peter Pan and never grow up. He said he was going to live with us forever. It was cute, and to be honest, he was such a joy that thinking about keeping him at 5 years old was a pleasant thought. But Josh didn't stay 5, and every year since then he's gotten one year older. He eventually realized he was growing up and embraced the idea. As he grew into his teen years he began—like all teenagers—to wonder and sometimes even worry about his future. Whether they verbalize the questions or not, teenagers are asking things like What should I do with my life? Do I need to go to college? If so, what career path will I pursue? Will I get a job? Will I like my job? Will I earn enough money? Where will I live? Will I get married? And so on. These questions are difficult and overwhelming, especially in a world that is ready to offer answers that are sometimes contrary to the way Jesus Christ calls his followers to live. Be sensitive to your teenagers as they face the task of deciding what to do with their lives. Help them to see that their search should leave them looking for answers from God and his Word, rather than from the world. Your input, guidance, and direction are not only valuable but will be valued by your teenagers.

76 JUST WHEN WE'RE TEMPTED TO SPEED IT UP, WE NEED TO SLOW IT DOWN.

OK, so you're wondering how quickly you can make these sometimes awkward and difficult years of adolescence pass. Guess what—your teenagers have that same hope, and it's not necessarily a healthy thing. Marketers understand this much better than we do as parents. They're well aware of the fact that our teenagers want to feel, look, be perceived, and be treated as older than they are. The gap between real-age and aspired-to-age narrows as kids get older. It's at its worst when they enter adolescence. Researchers have discovered that 12- and 13-year-olds aspire to be 17. Fourteen- to 16-year-olds aspire to be 19. And 17- to 19-year-olds aspire to be 20. This reality offers a partial explanation for why you may hear "Stop treating me like a child!" While we should always treat our teenagers in age-appropriate ways with dignity and respect, we don't want to cave in and go too fast. Slow it down when you see your children caving in to age-aspiration in ways that are dangerous, inappropriate, and wrong. Don't let them grow up too fast or too soon.

MAKE SURE THEY'RE GETTING ENOUGH SLEEP.

The old stereotype of the lazy teenager is the kid who needs to be prodded—several times—to get out of bed before noon. But in today's world, that stereotype usually doesn't hold up. Because their lives are filled with juggling a host of responsibilities and activities, our teenagers are shortchanging themselves on sleep. Add to that the fact that many teenagers are staying up or waking up to send and receive text messages, and the problem is compounded. God made our bodies to thrive when the cycle of waking and resting is maintained in healthy and balanced ways. Because their bodies are growing and forming, teenagers need to average about nine hours of sleep a night. Maybe you need to prod your teenager *into*—rather than *out of*—bed.

FACING YOUR FEARS

78 HEY, THIS AIN'T EASY!

Where in the world did we ever pick up the notion that everything in life *should* come easy—especially for those who follow Jesus? Have you ever taken the time to read the Bible carefully? God's people always encountered difficulty. In fact, when Jesus invites people to "come and follow me," there's a cross to carry. Raising and relating to children is difficult work. It gets even more difficult when they hit the adolescent years. Living with and raising teenagers is an experience full of great joy *and* great difficulty. You will struggle at times as a parent. Know that you are not alone. Our parenting story is one littered with our own feelings of inadequacy. We've struggled with rebellion. We've known frustration, disappointment, sickening dread, sleepless nights, and deep sadness. We've wavered between tenderness and contempt. The reality is that parenting teenagers isn't easy. However, we can and must approach our God-given role as a parent as a glorious challenge and opportunity.

79 YOU MUST FACE YOUR PARENTING FEARS.

Do you ever look at your children and get scared? Be assured, you're not alone. We've been there. It is sometimes paralyzing to think about parenting teenager who are growing through unbelievable amounts of change, while they're engaging with a rapidly changing and frightening world. In some ways this is nothing new. Did you ever hear what Mark Twain said about teenagers? "When a child turns 12 you should put him in a barrel, nail the lid down, and feed him through a knot hole. When he turns 16, plug the hole!" I once had an adult tell me that watching the kids in his neighborhood go through the teenage years was the most effective method of birth control around. But should we be afraid? While parents should be cautious, watchful, and discerning, we can't allow ourselves to fall victim to fear. If we become fearful, we might be tempted to remove our children from the world, believing that doing so will keep them from harm. Wholesale removal is never possible. And besides, it doesn't prepare our teenagers to live *for* Christ *in* the world. Fear can also immobilize us as parents, keeping us from constructively responding to and addressing the things our children face on a daily basis. Ever heard of paralyzing fear? Jesus has conquered fear and sent his promised Holy Spirit to comfort and guide us. As the parents of teenagers, we've learned that the comforting words the angel of the Lord spoke to shepherds keeping watch over their flocks by night are words for us: "Do not be afraid."

CONFUSED? FRIGHTENED? NOT SURE WHAT TO DO? MAYBE YOU NEED TO KEEP THE LIGHT ON.

Now that I'm in my 50s, I've got enough of a history to know that life is a journey that can be pretty intimidating and confusing. Having kids brings that reality home. As one parent half-seriously said to me, "There are the parenting years that go real well. And then there are the years of parenting teenagers." To be honest, it's the gift of difficulty and confusion that we need to redirect our eyes, ears, minds, and hearts to where they should be aimed. In a world that makes it easy to look for guidance and direction in all the wrong places, we're prone to follow a host of "guiding lights" that wind up leading us in the wrong direction. In a world where there are many "experts" sharing conflicting opinions on how to parent our kids through the teenage years, it's good to know there's a light we can trust. And the One who created life, children, teenagers, parents, and families offers that light to us. That light is the Word—both the incarnate Word, Jesus Christ, and the written Word. Together, the example of Christ and God's revelation of himself in the Bible reveals what we need to know and the paths we need to take during every step of the journey. As a child, I remember memorizing the words of Psalm 119:105 in Sunday school: *Your word is a lamp to guide my feet and a light for my path.* Want to know how the Bible can help you as a parent? It offers trustworthy instruction. It offers a plumb line for evaluating the glut of guidance we receive on parenting in today's world. It tells us where we've gone wrong and how to correct course. And it lays out a clear path for right and God-honoring parenting. Parenting teenagers is sometimes like finding your way through the dark woods in the middle of the night. It can't be done without a flashlight.

81 DON'T BASE YOUR HAPPINESS ON YOUR TEENAGERS' HAPPINESS.

If you do, you're just setting yourself up for disappointment. We've learned that even though we began our parenting adventure with a wonderfully written script—a script written by us that looked quite a bit like a Norman Rockwell painting—God had a different script for us to live. His script wasn't 100 percent happy like ours.

While it was a struggle for us, we learned that God gives us and our children the opportunity to struggle through life so that we might grow and mature. If we based our happiness on how well things were going with our kids—well, we'd all wind up spending time being miserable people. The Apostle Paul laid out a better way—in fact, it's the right way. He writes: *Base your happiness on your hope in Christ. When trials come endure them patiently; steadfastly maintain the habit of prayer (Romans 12:12 Phillips).*

82 OVERWHELMED AND STRESSED? GET HELP.

Sometimes the circumstances in our own lives and the stresses of raising and living with teenagers can become overwhelming, paralyzing, and detrimental to our spiritual and emotional well-being. When that happens, we're not doing anyone any favors if we continue to spiral down out of control. If our normal support systems aren't enough to carry us through, then it's time to seek some outside help—maybe even some professional counseling. One or two sessions with a trained and competent Christian counselor may be enough to provide you with the guidance and support you need to get back on the right course. Perhaps long-term counseling is needed. Ask your pastor or a trusted friend to recommend a Christian counselor. Going to counseling *isn't* an admission that you're weak. A counselor can offer an unbiased perspective, help you identify contributing factors, assist in self-examination, and give you guidance in making decisions that will lead to wholeness and healing.

83 MAJOR ON THE MAJORS.

Tattoos, piercings, hairstyles, clothes—these are some of the things we tend to make into major conflict points in our families. For example, when generational styles collide, we tend to turn personal taste and style issues into moral issues in an effort to keep our teenagers from altering their appearance in a way that we either find embarrassing or wrong. Like it or not, teenagers have always had their own unique styles that allow them to identify as a distinct group away from previous generations. If you don't believe it, just go back and leaf through your high school yearbook. Add to the issue of style the fact that they tend to try on different "selves" in the quest to discover their identity, and there's fertile ground for parent-teen conflict. On the one hand, these are issues and matters that we must address with our children. But our first task in this process is to discern the roots of the behaviors. If their fascination with these things isn't symptomatic of a deeper heart issue, then we shouldn't prohibit things that the Scriptures don't prohibit or label as wrong. Chances are, they'll eventually grow out of it and look back on what they did, asking the same question we ask when we look at our yearbooks: "What in the world was I thinking?" But if we discover there are heart issues that need to be addressed, then it's worth our while and time to intervene, set limits, and maybe even save them from their youthful selves. The old parenting cliché is worth remembering: "Major on the majors, not the minors."

84 DON'T WORRY ABOUT WHAT OTHERS THINK OR KNOW.

Remember what used to happen to the teenage girl from the Christian family who got pregnant? Maybe you don't, because you never heard in the first place that the girl was even pregnant. She just disappeared—usually halfway across the country to Aunt Martha's farm. Then, a year or two later, she'd reappear and life would go on as if nothing happened. That's the way it used to be in the church when a family was in crisis. If other people found out, a family was surrounded by judgment rather than grace. We deal with the fallout of that way of life when we find ourselves in crisis and our first thought is "What will other people think?" or "Who knows?" Consequently, we do all we can to cover up the crisis, deal with it quietly, and move on. But that's a horrible way to live, and it's not the least bit helpful to our children. It exposes the idolatry of our own hearts, sending the message that we're more concerned about what other people think of us than the well-being of our children. It robs us and the church of the opportunity to minister and be ministered to. It limits the much-needed prayer support that carries us through a crisis. And it teaches our teenagers that we should hide our sin rather than deal with it.

In our family, crisis times are times when we immediately get on the phone or fire out e-mails to those close to us who we know will love us, support us, pray for us, and walk with us through our crisis. Who cares what other people think?

PRESSURES

85 MEDIA POUNDS THEM WITH APPEARANCE PRESSURE.

Remember the amount of time you spent looking in the mirror when you were a teenager? Come on, admit it. I know I'm not the only who looked at myself from every possible angle. We wondered what was happening, wondered where it was all going, and usually lamented that we weren't "shaping up" the way we thought we should. It's still the same for today's teenagers— but then again, it's also very different. When they look in the mirror at themselves, they're also looking over their shoulders at the images of the perfect people the media throw at them thousands of times a day—actors, actresses, supermodels, sports stars, and other celebrities and notables. Somewhere along the way, our teenagers believe the lie that if you want to be valuable, worthwhile, lovable, and acceptable, then that's what you must look like. They struggle with who they are because of who they've been led to believe they *should* be. By being loving, sensitive, and resistant to these pressures in your own life, you can serve as a buffer in the midst of a pressure-filled media and peer culture that relentlessly hammers teenagers with these dangerous and impossible-to-achieve standards.

86 IF IT'S A BIG DEAL TO THEM, IT'S A BIG DEAL.

The amount of change and questioning our teenagers face makes them more vulnerable to stress than any other age group. Things that would never bother us as adults can be devastating to a teenager. The stuff we might write off or not even cause a bother can be monumentally difficult for them to handle or overcome. When you've seen a teenager stress out over a "wardrobe crisis," mediocre test grade that has no bearing on eternity, or facial blemish, you have to wonder what might happen if he or she would ever face problems of a more severe and significant nature. We can't forget that the adolescent years are a time of change, pressure, crisis, and even impulsive overreaction. Teenagers tend to center on the crisis of the moment, no matter how large or small that crisis may seem to us. Our goal shouldn't be to write the crisis off as silly or insignificant. While we might be tempted to simply say "get over it" (and there are times where that response might be justified), it's better to walk through the crisis with them and allow them to express themselves, all the while offering support and the benefit of a more mature perspective.

TEACH THEM HOW TO SUFFER WELL.

Living in a feelings-oriented culture conditions us to avoid pain and pursue pleasure. Our teenagers are no different. When life gets hard, they look for the button to push, the pill to take, or the principle to enact that will make things right. Like us, they look for easy and quick solutions to their problems. But the best way for us to prepare them for life is to teach them three simple biblical truths. First, pain and suffering in this life are inescapable. There's no avoiding it. Second, pain and suffering are temporary. At times, God brings relief in this life. At other times, relief may not come until the day we pass from our earthly to our heavenly lives—a day when heartache and despair will be no more. And third, God alone is our source of strength during times of suffering. Jesus told his followers to expect pain and persecution. The psalms are full of lament over life's difficulties. Remember the familiar words of Psalm 46:1? *God is our refuge and strength, always ready to help in times of trouble.* Our words and example should teach our children how to handle life's difficulties in full reliance and dependence on God.

88   HOLD THEM LIKE SOAP.

I once heard that raising teenagers is like holding a wet bar of soap: Too firm a grasp, and it shoots from your hand; too loose a grasp, and it slides away. A gentle but firm grasp keeps it in your hand. One of the greatest gifts we can give to our children is the gift of reasonable and loving boundaries. Boundaries help our teenagers to recognize right from wrong, to stay safe within the confines of God's will and way, and to teach them the self-control that will serve them well as they take on responsibility for themselves for the rest of their lives. When your adult children look back on their growing-up years, they will thank you for taking the time to teach them that there truly is right and wrong in a world that works so hard to teach them otherwise.

COMMUNICATION

89 LISTEN—AND LISTEN HARD— BEFORE YOU SPEAK.

This one's been a big struggle for me. All too often I'm the guy who's described in Proverbs 18. I'm one of those fools who *have no interest in understanding; they only want to air their own opinions* (v. 2) and the shameful fool who speaks *before listening to the facts* (v. 13). I've had to learn the hard way that when I've been thrust into conversations with my teenagers where we don't see eye-to-eye, it's sometimes best to bite my tongue, shut my mouth, and open my ears. We have to remember that our teenagers are not yet adults. We can expect a mix of their developing and not-yet-there thinking ability to be tainted by immaturity, impulsivity, inconsistent logic, and a lack of the kind of wisdom that comes with age and experience. Speaking quickly to point out that (a) they have no idea what they're talking about, (b) they're wrong, and (c) here's the right answer—

well, you know where that goes. Listen first. And when they know they've been heard and respected, they're more prone to hear our carefully crafted and well-thought-out response.

90 NEVER FORGET TO SAY THE TWO THINGS THEY LOVE TO HEAR.

No, it's not "Congratulations! You're 13 and you can now do whatever you want!"—nor is it "Happy 16th birthday and here are the keys to your brand-new car!" What teenagers have consistently told me over the years is that there are two things their parents say that make them very, very happy: "I love you" and "I'm proud of you." You can never say either enough.

91 ASK GOOD QUESTIONS.

Our tendency is to talk at rather than listen to our teenagers. The bad news is that this approach is a communication killer. Asking good questions serves to open the floodgates of communication by encouraging your teenagers to express themselves. Asking questions lets them know you want to hear what they have to say. Good questions asked at just the right time help teenagers think through their actions, process the decisions they've made, and consider the resulting consequences. Good questions give teenagers the opportunity to be treated like adults rather than young children. And remember, good questions are differentiated from bad questions because they can't be answered with only one word or a grunt. Good open-ended questions start with words like *how*, *why*, and *what*.

92 TELL YOUR TEENAGE STORY.

"How much should I tell my kids about my life as a teenager?" Ever wonder about that one? You have if you're conscious about the mistakes you made during your teenage years and you're dreading the day one of your children starts asking those uncomfortable and probing questions. And you've wondered in those awkward moments when your child asks things like "Hey, Dad...hey, Mom...did you ever _____?"(Fill in the blank with a questionable behavior!) Awkward, isn't it? Answering with age-appropriate honesty is the best policy when teenagers are considering their own actions and wondering about what you did when you were their age. Our children have asked us some very frank questions over the years. And we've given them some very frank answers. At times, we've been able to espouse the virtues of God's ways by speaking from the experience of embracing those ways during our own teenage years. At other times, we've been able to espouse the virtues of God's ways by talking openly about the sins of our past and the resulting consequences of those sins. Telling your story with honesty is helpful for your teenagers, and your vulnerability makes you a real and credible person in their eyes. By admitting our mistakes, we model the truths of the Gospel, our need for a redeemer, and the life-giving freedom of forgiveness our children so desperately need to experience and understand.

93 CHOOSE YOUR WORDS CAREFULLY.

Proverbs 12:18 tells us: *Some people make cutting remarks, but the words of the wise bring healing.* I read that and can only respond with one word: "Guilty!" In my relationships, I've thrown around reckless words and cutting remarks with abandon, especially with those who live under my roof. Reckless words are not only harmful to our communication but also to our relationships with our children. Stuff that mindlessly rolls off our tongues in a rage-filled or careless moment can stick with them forever. Taking the time to habitually think before we speak is an investment that will pay great dividends in strengthened parent-teen relationships and positive parental influence.

94 SEIZE EVERY OPPORTUNITY FOR CONVERSATION.

Don't ever stop trying to engage in conversation with your teenagers. Because their lives are busy and they are spending increasing amounts of time outside of your home and away from you, the opportunities to communicate like you once did will wane. As that happens, go out of your way to make the most of the moments you share together before they leave for school, when they arrive home, when you're sharing a meal, when you're in the car together, or before they head to bed.

FRIENDS/ PEERS

95 GET TO KNOW THEIR FRIENDS.

Because the teenage years are filled with so much change and uncertainty, your children yearn for stability and normalcy. Their search for a safe place to belong leads them to the haven of friendships with peers. These friendships are important and necessary as our teenagers begin to move toward the independence of adulthood. This means they'll face peer pressure. That pressure can either be positive (influencing them to make good choices), or negative—something most of us remember all too well from the impulsive peer-influenced decisions we made during own teenage years! Getting to know your teenagers' friends opens a wide window into understanding the unique blend of peer pressures your children are facing. That knowledge allows you to respond to those realities with Christ-like wisdom, direction, and boundaries. But that's not all. You'll be opening the door to other teenagers who will benefit from—and might even desperately need—your friendship, adult wisdom, and guidance as well.

96 A PLACE—THAT'S WHAT THEY WANT TO FIND.

The hallway of my junior high school seemed less like a passageway from class to class and more like a gantlet. Walking that hallway was painful business as my self-conscious self wondered where—if anywhere—I fit in to that mass of same-aged students known as my peers. Some things never change. As children move into the early stages of adolescence, peers become increasingly important. Teenagers feel more secure when they are accepted by a group of friends. Hiding in the confines of a group offers safety to an insecure and self-conscious teenager. Peer acceptance is sometimes pursued with reckless abandon—and what they often abandon are the beliefs and behaviors you've instilled in them as decent, good, and right. Because rejection is feared and to be avoided at all costs, many teenagers will compromise these standards of right and wrong if that compromise will facilitate peer acceptance rather than rejection. As a result, your teenagers may "try on" a number of different peer groups until they find what they think is a good fit. Changes in attitude, dress, and conduct might accompany their trips to and from the peer group "fitting room." While this "normal" behavior doesn't always result in doing what's right, it is a time during which teenagers learn how to choose friends. It's also a prime time to give your input on peer pressure, decision-making, God-honoring choices, and the nature of healthy friendships.

REMEMBER PEER PRESSURE? IT'S STILL HERE—BUT VERY DIFFERENT.

Negative peer pressure use to take the form of a verbal invitation to get involved in some kind of behavior that both you and the person inviting you knew was wrong. That's why we spent so much time sneaking around, looking over our shoulders, whispering, and trying not to get caught! If only peer pressure was so easy (relatively!) for our teenagers. But they live in a different world. Think carefully about this—in today's world, negative peer pressure usually takes the form of an *unspoken expectation* to get involved in something that the great majority of the peer group thinks is *normal* and *right*. Do you know what that's like for your teenagers? It makes peer pressure that much harder to resist. Since everyone is doing it and nobody thinks it's wrong—well, it must be OK. And by the way, that means there's no longer a need to sneak around. This makes it imperative that we as parents set clear standards of right and wrong, set clear guidelines for the consequences of stepping over the boundaries, and enforce those consequences. But even before that, we need to build strong give-and-take relationships with our children marked by grace and love. That's the kind of stuff that builds in the resilience that helps your teenagers recognize right from wrong and have the courage to say no in the first place.

98 MAKE YOUR HOME A REFUGE.

Life for teenagers is difficult. When their hands hit the doorknob at your house, do they feel like they are stepping out of a difficult world into a place of even greater heartache, brokenness, and difficulty? Or are they able to breathe a sigh of relief as they step over the threshold into the loving, safe, and comforting place they call home? Be sure your home is the latter. And once it is, why not open the doors to your teenager's peers, providing them with a safe and welcoming place, too? Chances are good that your teenager has friends whose homes are anything but peaceful. Don't see the presence of these teenagers as a burden. Rather, embrace the opportunity to love an adolescent who may not experience love anywhere else. If this is what you hope for your home to become, why not refinish your basement or furnish another room with a mind toward filling it with teenagers? Fill your refrigerator with food and drinks (nonalcoholic!) for them.

The potential for making a positive impact in a teenager's life is tremendous.

AND FINALLY ...

99 DON'T TRUST CHRISTIAN PARENTING BOOKS.

I know what you're thinking now: "If I had known that I would never have thought about buying or reading this book!" But before you jump to that conclusion, how about an explanation? The problems we've found with Christian parenting books are that all too often they offer readers a foolproof formula for raising spiritually healthy and wealthy kids. Sorry, but it doesn't work that way. Or they've been written by people who have either not yet been involved in the process of raising their children through the teenage years, or maybe they don't even have children of their own. Sure, these people can pass on wisdom, but most of what we've read in those books seems a bit arrogant or condescending. Most Christian parenting books leave readers feeling hopeless or beat up. We'll admit that saying "Don't trust Christian parenting books" is an overstatement, but it is a thought we've had. Since our hope is that this little book has served you as a teaser to get you thinking and reading more on what it means to parent teenagers, we would like to recommend three Christian parenting books that are realistic, vulnerable, biblically faithful, hopeful, and very helpful. We recommend these books everywhere we go. The first two are Paul David Tripp's *Age of Opportunity: A Biblical Guide to Parenting Teens* and Leslie Leyland Fields' *Parenting Is Your Highest Calling: And 8 Other Myths That Trap Us in Worry and Guilt*. The third is a book for Christian parents who are struggling through a difficult relationship with a prodigal son or daughter: *Come Back, Barbara* by C. John Miller and Barbara Miller Juliani.